C000226079

A BOOK OF
ENGLISH TRADES

Copper-Plate Printer

A BOOK OF
ENGLISH
TRADES

BEING
A LIBRARY OF THE
USEFUL ARTS

ENGLISH HERITAGE

Published by English Heritage, NMRC, Kemble Drive,
Swindon SN2 2GZ
www.english-heritage.org.uk

First published by English Heritage 2006
© English Heritage 2006

ISBN-10   1 85074 978 7
ISBN-13   978 1 85074 978 3
Product code 51111

A CIP catalogue for this book is available from the
British Library

Selected and abridged by Elizabeth Drury
Designed by Eric Drewery
Printed in Hong Kong

FOREWORD

Between 1804 and 1805, three separate volumes of 'The Book of Trades or Library of the Useful Arts' were printed for Tabart and Co., of 157 New Bond Street, London. They sold for three shillings each, or five shillings with beautifully coloured plates.

They were placed in Tabart's shop among the school and juvenile books. As was explained in later editions, the text and pictures — now published in a single volume — were designed to acquaint the rising generation with the various trades that they might pursue.

A brazier needs strength as well as ingenuity, the young adult is informed, while no great strength is required to become a tin-plate worker or a weaver. A journeyman plumber will earn about thirty shillings a week, compared with a stocking weaver, who with application could earn more than a guinea and a half a week; a painter is paid according to his talents and the celebrity he has acquired. The tailor must be able, 'not only to cut for the handsome and well-shaped, but bestow a good shape where nature has not granted it'. Women are employed to make watch-chains and polish buttons, and generally form part of a gang of brick-makers – together with two children.

The techniques and labours involved in the various crafts and trades were described and pictured for the young people who would constitute the skilled workers of late Georgian and Victorian England.

The text of this edition is reprinted and abridged from the seventh edition of 1818; the engraved illustrations are reproduced from this and the twelfth edition of 1839.

Spinner

THE APOTHECARY

The office of *Apothecary* is to attend on sick persons, and to prepare and to give them medicines, either on his own judgment, or according to the prescription of the Physician.

The Apothecaries, as a body, have a hall near Bridge Street, Blackfriars, where there are two magnificent laboratories, out of which all the surgeons are supplied with medicines for the British Navy. Here also, drugs of all sorts are sold to the public, which may be depended upon as pure and unadulterated. They are obliged to make up their medicines according to the formulas prescribed in the Dispensary of the Royal College of Physicians, and are liable to have their shops visited by censors of the College, who are employed to destroy such medicines as they think not good.

In many places, and particularly in opulent cities, the first Apothecaries' shops were established at the public expense, and belonged in fact to the magistrates. A particular garden also was often appropriated to the use of the Apothecary, in order that he might rear in it the necessary plants.

Apothecary

THE BAKER

The business of the Baker consists in making bread, rolls, and biscuits, and in baking various kinds of provisions.

Bread is made of flour, mixed and kneaded with yeast, water, and a little salt; the salt making the bread more perfect by being dissolved in water, the fluid penetrating the flour in the most intimate manner; by which the bread becomes more light, better tasted, and will keep a longer time. It is known in London under two names, the white, or wheaten, and the household: these differ only in degree of purity; and the loaves must be marked with a W, or H, or the baker is liable to suffer a penalty.

The life of a baker is very laborious; the greater part of the work being done by night: the journeyman is required always to commence his operations about eleven o'clock in the evening, in order to get the new bread ready for admitting the rolls in the morning. His wages are, however, but very moderate, seldom amounting to more than ten shillings a week, exclusive of his board.

Baker

THE BASKET-MAKER

Baskets are made either of rushes, splinters, or willows, which last are, according to their growth, called osiers or sallows. They thrive best in moist places.

The business of a basket-maker requires but a small capital, either of money or ingenuity, in consequence of which, it has been fixed upon as one of the most proper occupations for that class of our suffering fellow-creatures, the indigent blind, for whom asylums are established in different cities of the empire, and where the art of basket-making is carried to a surprising degree of perfection. Besides affording the pupils instruction gratis, these asylums allow them a weekly sum, proportioned to the nature of their work, and the proficiency made by them, thereby relieving them, in some degree at least, from the painful idea of absolute dependence on the bounty of others; and, which is of scarcely less importance, affording them an active employment for those hours which would be otherwise spent in despondency and gloom.

Basket-maker

THE BOOKSELLER

The Bookseller of the present day is a person of considerable importance in the republic of letters, more especially if he combines those particular branches of the trade denominated *Proprietor* and *Publisher*: for it is to such men our men of genius take their productions for sale: and the success of works of genius very frequently depends upon their spirit, probity, and patronage. It is also to such men that the reading public generally are indebted for almost every important work of a voluminous kind. Those bulky and valuable volumes, the various Encyclopædias, would never have made their appearance had not a Bookseller, or a combination of Booksellers, entered upon the speculation by employing men of science and learning in the various departments of those works, and embarking large capitals in the undertaking.

Paternoster Row has been, for a long period, notorious as the place in which some of these large establishments are carried on, and where a great number of Booksellers' shops and warehouses abound.

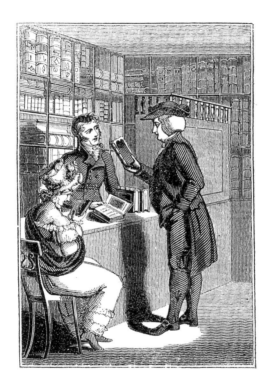

Bookseller

THE BRAZIER

The Brazier makes kettles, pans, candle-sticks, and other kitchen utensils, of brass, which is not a simple metal, but compounded of copper and zinc, in certain proportions: if the proportion of copper be greater, the compound is pinch-beck. Copper alloyed with tin, makes bronze, bell-metal, &c.

Brass is capable of being wrought with very great facility, and is applied to a variety of purposes of the arts. It is of a beautiful yellow-colour, more approaching to that of gold, and not so apt to tarnish or rust, as copper. It is more ductile than either that metal or iron; and hence, peculiarly fitted to be made into wire.

Some of the articles manufactured by the working brazier, are beat out with the hammer, and united in their several parts by solder; others are cast: those which are cast, belong to the business of the founder, except the polishing and finishing, which require the art of the brazier.

The working brazier has need of strength, and if he would excel in his business, he should possess ingenuity to finish the work with taste.

Brazier

THE BREWER

Different counties of England are celebrated for their peculiar ales, and London porter is famous in almost all parts of the civilized world. Different as these several sorts of liquor are, they are nevertheless, for the most part, composed of the same materials variously prepared.

Malt liquor, in general, is composed of water, malt, hops, and a little yeast; and the great art is to find out the proper proportions of each ingredient, to what degree of heat the water must be raised before it is poured on the malt, and how best to work it afterwards.

The first part of the operation is called *mashing*, which is performed in a large circular vessel, such as that represented in the upper part of the plate.

Common report says, that in addition to malt and hops, a variety of other ingredients are used, and none of them of the most wholesome nature.

The lower part of the plate represents the brew-house yard, with the casks ready to be taken away by the carman.

Brewer

THE BRICKLAYER

Bricklaying is the art of cementing bricks, by lime or some other cement, so as to form one body; hence its use and importance in building walls, houses, &c.

Bricklayers are supplied with bricks and mortar, by a man they call a *labourer*, who is also employed in making the mortar from lime. The labourer brings the mortar and the bricks in a machine called a hod, which he carries on his shoulder. Before he puts the mortar into the hod, he throws over every part of the inner surface, fine dry sand, to prevent it from sticking to the wood.

A Bricklayer and his labourer will lay in a single day about a thousand bricks, in what is called whole and solid work, when the wall is either a brick and a half or two bricks thick; and since a cubic yard contains 460 bricks, he will lay above two cubic yards in a day.

Bricklayers compute new work, such as the walls of houses, &c. by the rod of 16 feet, and the price charged includes the putting up and use of scaffolding; but the clearing out and carrying away the rubbish, is an extra charge.

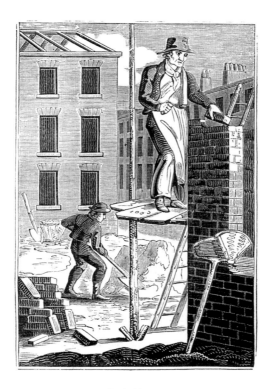

Bricklayer

THE BRICK-MAKER

The business of a Brick-maker is carried on in the open fields, and its mode of operation may be seen in the neighbourhood of most large towns. The art, in almost all its branches, is regulated by different acts of parliament: and Bricks may be made of pure clay, or clay mixed in certain proportions with sand or ashes.

The clay is first moistened, and tempered with water, either by the feet, or by means of a machine or mill worked with one or more horses.

When it is fit for moulding into Bricks, several persons are usually, in the neighbourhood of London, employed upon the business of making a single Brick; these are called gangs: they consist of one or two men, a woman, and two children, to each of which is assigned a different department in the occupation. A gang in full work will make many thousand Bricks in a day.

In the plate the man only is represented in the act of moulding the clay into the shape of a Brick: he stands under a sort of thatched cover to keep off the sun and the rain.

Brick-maker

THE BRUSH-MAKER

The nature of this man's business is very well displayed in the plate. He makes brushes, hair and carpet brooms, and mops of all sorts; he is generally the manufacturer of wooden coal-hods, and of measures for corn and coals.

The wooden part of brushes is generally of oak or elm, which is cut to its proper size by the instrument which the man in the figure is supposed to be using. The instrument is a large knife, fastened down to the block with a staple at one end, in such a manner, that it is moveable up and down; to the other end is a handle. The wood to be cut, is held in the left hand, while the knife is worked with the right. The knife is always kept very sharp; and by its make and mode of using, hard wood is very readily reduced to any shape and size. This wood, when cut into the proper sizes, is drilled with as many holes as is necessary, and into these the hair is put.

The hair made use of by brush-makers, is hog's bristle, vast quantities of which are imported every year from Germany and Russia, when we are not at war with those powers.

Brush-maker

THE BUTTON-MAKER

Buttons are articles of dress serving to fasten clothes tight about the body. There are several kinds of buttons; some are made of gold and silver lace, others of mohair, silk, horse-hair, thread, metal, glass, &c.

Metal buttons are principally made in Birmingham.

The process is very simple after the metal comes out of the founder's hands. The pieces of metal are either cast or cut to the proper size, and then sent to the button-maker, who has dies or stamps according to the pattern wanted. The machine by which they are stamped is well exhibited in the plate. The man stands in a place lower than the floor, by which he is nearer on a level with the place on which his dies stand. By means of a single pulley he raises a weight, to the lower part of which is fixed another die; he lets the weight fall down on the metal, which effects his object. After this operation they are to be shanked, which is performed by means of solder; they are then polished by women.

Button-maker

THE CABINET-MAKER

As a first step, we should recommend to the student the practice of drawing from any good models, but more particularly from subjects connected with architecture.

An acquaintance with perspective is no less useful than a knowledge of drawing: for it is sometimes necessary, not only to delineate the particular articles of furniture, but to shew the effect it is likely to produce, when placed in the apartment for which it is designed.

The Cabinet-maker, represented in the plate, is one who makes chairs, tables, looking-glass frames, book-cases, &c. His chief tools are saws, axes, planes, chisels, files, gimblets, turn-screws, hammers, and other implements, which are used in common by the Carpenter and Cabinet-maker. The workman, represented in the plate, is in the act of making a looking-glass frame; he is putting some glue on one of the side pieces in order to fix it in the hole that is prepared to receive it.

The goodness and value of furniture depends on the fineness of the wood and other materials of which it is made, and on the neatness of the workmanship.

Cabinet-maker

THE CARPENTER

The art of the *Carpenter* is employed in framing and joining pieces of timber, and fitting them up in houses and other buildings, as well as in numerous other employments of a similar kind.

The Carpenter stands in need of a great variety of tools, such as saws, planes, chisels, hammers, hatchets, axes, awls, gimblets, &c. Common workmen are obliged to find their own tools, a set of which is worth from ten to twenty pounds, or even more. But for different kinds of mouldings, for beads, and fancy work, the master Carpenter supplies his men with the necessary implements.

The practices in the art of Carpentry and Joinery, are called planing, sawing, mortising, scribing, moulding, gluing, &c.

He is represented preparing boards to lay upon the roof of a new house in the background. The rafters are already in their places: the boards are to be laid next, in order to receive the slates.

A journeyman Carpenter, when he works by time, receives from three shillings and sixpence, to four shillings and sixpence a day.

Carpenter

THE COOPER

A Cooper manufactures casks, tubs, pails, and various other articles in domestic concerns, as well as vessels for carrying and transporting all kinds of liquids, and many dry wares.

After the staves are dressed, and ready to be arranged, the Cooper, without attempting any great nicety in sloping or beveling them, so that the *whole* surface of the edge may touch in every point, brings them into contact only at the inner surface, and then, by driving the hoops tight, he can make a closer joint than could be done by sloping the staves from the outer to the inner side. These staves are kept together by means of hoops, which are made of hazel and ash; but some articles require iron hoops.

The Cooper derives large profit, and great part of his employment, from the West-India trade. The puncheons and hogsheads are used in the voyage out to the Islands, for packing coarse goods, as coarse woollen cloths, coarse hats, &c. whence those vessels return filled with rum and sugar.

Cooper

THE GARDENER

The Gardener, who may be called a refined agriculturalist, is one who is engaged in the management and cultivation of fruit-trees, shrubs, flowers, plants, and vegetables of all kinds.

There are several kind of Gardeners; some gain a living by looking after other people's gardens; for which they receive a certain sum per annum, according to the size of the garden. Others, live in gentlemen's houses, and, like domestics in general, receive wages for their labour, from twenty, to a hundred pounds per annum, according to their merit, or to what may be expected of them. Some Gardeners go out to day-work, whose wages are from three to five shillings a day.

Besides these, we have Market-Gardeners, that is, persons who raise vegetables and fruit, which they expose to sale in markets and other places. Gardens, for the raising of vegetables for sale, were first cultivated about Sandwich in Kent. The example was soon followed near the metropolis.

Gardener

THE GLASS-BLOWER

Glass is a transparent, solid, brittle substance, formed by the combination of flint or silex, with alkaline salts and metallic oxides.

The furnace in which the glass is melted, is round, and has several apertures, in one of which the fuel is introduced; the others serve to lade out the melted metal.

When the ingredients are perfectly fused, and have acquired the necessary degree of heat, part of the melted matter is taken out at the end of a hollow tube, about two feet and a half long, which is dipped into it, and turned about till a sufficient quantity is taken up; the workman then rolls it gently upon a piece of iron to unite it more intimately. He then, as it is represented in the plate, blows through the tube till the melted mass at the extremity swells into a bubble; after which, he again rolls it on a smooth surface to polish it, and repeats the blowing till the glass is brought as near the size and form of the vessel required.

Glass-makers usually work in the cold months, owing to the great heat of their furnaces.

Glass-blower

THE IRON-FOUNDER

The uses to which cast iron was applied previously to the last century, are, comparatively, of trivial importance: it now enters more or less into the materials of almost every manufactory, forming wheels, cylinders, pipes, arches, grates, stoves, amid innumerable other appendages and implements, without which, the mechanic would be almost undone, and the domestic concerns of mankind would suffer considerable disadvantage and inconvenience.

The Founder has just taken from the furnace, a ladle full of liquid metal, with which he is going to cast, perhaps, the front of a stove, or some other article, the form of which is moulded out in stiff sand.

Cast-iron is now employed in the formation of bridges of great extent; in roofs, and the girders, and joists in buildings, as well as the sash-frames, and sashes. It has also been used with success in wheels and other machinery to our steam-engines. Birmingham and its neighbourhood, is the great entrepôt for works of all kinds in iron.

Iron-founder

THE JEWELLER

The name Jeweller, is now commonly applied to all who set stones, whether real or artificial; but, properly speaking, it belongs only to those who set diamonds and other precious gems. According to the general application of the term, Jewellers make rings of all sorts in gold, lockets, bracelets, broaches, ornaments for the head, ear-rings, necklaces, and a great variety of trinkets composed of diamonds, pearls, or other stones.

In the print we have a man at work, who will represent either a jeweller or a small worker in silver; one who makes rings, perfume boxes, &c. The board at which he works, is adapted, also, for a second workman. The leathern skins fastened to the board, are to catch the filings, and small pieces of precious metals which would otherwise be liable to fall on the ground.

On his left-hand, above the board, is a *drill-bow*; this is a flexible instrument consisting of a piece of steel, to the end of which is fastened a cat-gut: the cat-gut is twisted round one of the drills which stand before the man.

Jeweller

THE LACE-MAKER

The Lace-maker is a person, commonly a woman, who makes a kind of open network of thread, silk, &c. of various widths and fineness, with a variety of figures intermixed, used most commonly for trimmings to ladies' dresses.

The best laces are now made at Mecklin, Brussels, and Ghent, Antwerp and Valenciennes, which still enrich the country around, and induce the farmers to cultivate flax on the poorest soils. In France, lace was made, formerly, in large quantities, in the convents.

In our own country the manufacture of lace is carried on to a greater extent and perfection in Buckinghamshire, than in any other part of the United Kingdom, particularly in the town and neighbourhood of Newport-Pagnel, which is a sort of mart for that article, and flourishes considerably by its means.

The Lace-Maker is represented in the plate busily engaged in her work in the open air, which, even in this country, is no uncommon sight during the summer months.

Lace-maker

THE MACHINIST

The Machinist who embodies in his profession the chief principles of Mechanics, and brings them into active use, is the follower of an occupation of very recent introduction amongst the social and useful arts.

It is obvious, that the person who carries on this business must be possessed of considerable ingenuity and great mechanical knowledge: his employment being of a very complicated kind. He requires the talents and experience of the joiner, the brass and iron founder, the smith and the turner, in their most extended variety. It is by uniting the powers of these several occupations into one, together with the great assortment of excellent tools which he unavoidably requires, that the Machinist is furnished with those facilities of manufacture which peculiarly belong to his employment.

The plate represents the Machinist's workshop: with the five mechanical powers, viz. the screw, the pulley, the wheel, the wedge, and the lever. There is, also, the turning lathe, the steam engine, and the saw mill.

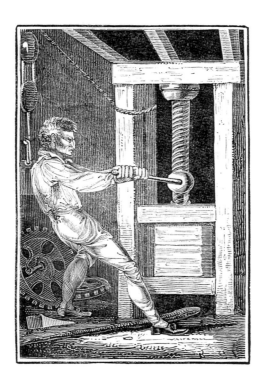

Machinist

THE MERCHANT

The Merchant is a wholesale dealer in all sorts of merchandise, who exports and imports goods to and from different parts of the world, who deals in exchange, and buys and sells goods in their original packages without breaking bulk.

To carry on the business of a Merchant with a high degree of credit, a man should possess a large stock of general knowledge, and a considerable capital; the one will prevent him from falling into errors, and the other will enable him to give credit to his customers both at home and abroad.

Merchants are distinguished from one another, either by the goods in which they traffic, or by the countries with which they have their chief correspondence.

To form an adequate idea of the mercantile transactions of the City of London alone, it has been computed that upon an average, about five thousand vessels sail from this port every year. These measure upwards of one million tons, and are navigated by about sixty thousand seamen.

Merchant

THE OPTICIAN

The Optician makes telescopes, microscopes, spectacles, opera-glasses, reading glasses, &c. &c.

Glass globes, and specula, seem to have been the only optical instruments known to the ancients. Alhazen gave the first hint of the invention of spectacles. From the writings of this author, together with the observations of Roger Bacon, it is not improbable that some monks gradually hit upon the construction of spectacles. It is certain that spectacles were well known in the 13th century, and not long before. It is said, that Alexander Spina, a native of Pisa, who died in 1313, happened to see a pair of spectacles in the hands of a person who would not explain them to him, and that he succeeded in making a pair for himself, and immediately made the construction public. It is also inscribed on the tomb of Salvinus Armatus, a nobleman of Florence, who died in 1317, that he was the inventor of spectacles.

The plate represents the Optician's shop, in which are seen the telescope, the microscope, spectacles, opera-glasses, &c.

Optician

THE PAINTER

The implements made use of in this art, are a stone and a muller to grind the colours; an operation which is sometimes performed with oil, and sometimes with water: hence, the distinction between *painting in oil* and painting in water colours. A palette and palette knife are also required; the *latter* to take off the paint from the stone, and the *former*, which is made of walnut-tree or mahogany, is that on which the artist puts his colours for immediate use. The pencils or brushes, are made of camel's hair, badger's hair, or hog's bristles.

The stick in the Painter's hand is about a yard long, with cotton wool tied round the end in a piece of soft leather to prevent its scratching the picture. On this the artist rests his right hand, to keep it steady. The canvas for the intended picture is placed on a wooden frame, called an *easel*, which is so constructed, by means of holes and pegs, that it may be raised or lowered at pleasure. The earnings of an artist cannot be defined: he is paid according to his talents, and to the celebrity he has acquired.

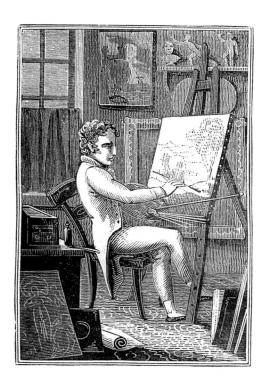

Painter

THE PEWTERER

Pewter is a factitious metal, and very uncertain in its composition. It is generally kept of different standards: that which is called plate-metal, is said to be formed of tin and regulus of antimony, in the proportions of 112 pounds of the former, to six or seven pounds of the latter.

The next inferior to this is called trifling metal, and is lowered by alloying it with lead: of this metal ale-house pots are made.

The moulds for flat pewter are composed of two pieces, one of which forms the upper, the other the under part of the article.

The moulds for pots, &c. are composed of four pieces, two for the bottom, and two for the sides. Before the moulds are used, it is necessary to rub them with fine coal dust, mixed with the white of an egg.

The plate represents the pewterer in the act of casting some article on a bench, with dishes, syringes, &c. around him: the pot in which is the melted metal, is on the ground by his side.

Pewterer

THE PLUMBER

The business of the Plumber consists in casting and working of lead, and using it in buildings. He furnishes us with a cistern for water, and with a sink for a kitchen; he covers the house with lead, and makes the gutters to carry away the water; he makes pipes of all sorts and sizes, and sometimes he casts leaden statues as ornaments for the garden. The plumber also is employed in making coffins for those who are to be interred out of the usual way. He also fits up water-closets and makes pumps.

In the country it is not infrequent to find that the business of a plumber, glazier, and painter, is united in the same person.

The health of the men is often injured by the fumes of the lead.

Journeymen earn about thirty shillings a week; and we recommend earnestly to lads brought up to either of the before-mentioned trades, that they cultivate cleanliness and strict sobriety, and that they never, on any account, eat their meals, or retire to rest at night, before they have well washed their hands and face.

Plumber

THE POTTER

The wheel and the lathe are the chief instruments in the business of the pottery: the first is intended for large works, and the other for small; the wheel is turned by a labourer, as represented in the plate; but the lathe is put into motion by the foot of the workman.

English stone-ware is made of tobacco-pipe clay mixed with flints calcined and ground. This mixture burns white, and vessels of this kind were formerly all glazed with sea salt. Wedgewood's queen's-ware is made of tobacco-pipe clay, much beaten in water. By this process the finer parts of the clay remain suspended in the water, while the coarser and all impurities fall to the bottom. The thick liquid is further purified by passing it through hair and lawn sieves, after which it is mixed with another liquid, consisting of flints, calcined, ground, and suspended in water. The mixture is then dried in a kiln; and being afterwards beaten to a proper temper, it becomes fit for being formed at a wheel into dishes, plates, bowls, &c.

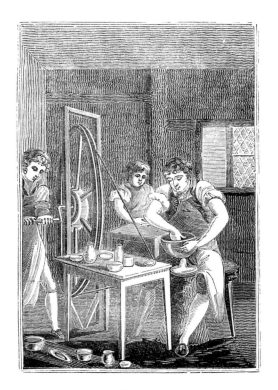

Potter

THE PRINTER

The workmen employed in printing are of two kinds: *compositors*, who range and dispose the letters into words, lines, pages, &c. according to the copy delivered to them by the author; and the *pressmen*, who apply ink upon the same, and take off the impression. In the back-ground of the plate a compositor is represented at work, and a pressman is engaged at his business in the front.

There are two cases for the purpose of containing the types, called the upper and the lower case. In the upper are placed, in separate boxes, or divisions, the capitals, small capitals, accented letters, figures, and the marks of reference; in the lower, are placed the small letters, also the double letters, the stops, and the spaces which go between the words and fill up short lines. A pair of cases for the Roman types, and another for the Italic, are usually placed on each side the frame, and they stand sloping in such a manner as that every part shall be within the reach of the compositor.

Printer

THE ROPE-MAKER

Ropes of all kinds are generally made of hemp, twisted or spun, something after the same manner as the spinning of wool; and the places in which ropes are made, are called rope-walks. These are sometimes a quarter of a mile or more in length, in the open air, and have a row or rows of trees planted beside them for shade, or are covered with a slight shed to keep the workmen from the inclemencies and changes of the weather.

At the upper-end of the rope-walk is a spinning-wheel, which is turned round by a person, who sits on a stool or bench for the purpose; the man who forms the rope or string, has a bundle of dressed hemp, such as that which lies on the truck in the plate, round his waist. From this he draws out two or more ends, and fixes them to a hook; the wheel is now turned, by which the threads are twisted, and as the spinner walks backward, the rope, or more properly the rope-yarn, is lengthened. The part already twisted draws along with it more fibres out of the bundle.

Rope-maker

THE SADDLER

A saddle consists of a wooden frame, called a saddle-tree, on which is laid a quantity of horse-hair, wool, &c. and this is covered over with tanned leather, neatly nailed to the wooden tree.

The tree-maker furnishes only the wooden part of the saddle; this is, however, a very important part of the business; because upon the saddle-tree the fitting of the saddle depends.

The saddler's iron-monger furnishes him with the iron or steel stirrups, buckles of all kinds, bits for bridles, and other steel or brass furniture required for the harness of a horse, either for riding or drawing in a carriage. Many of these articles are originally made by the iron-founder.

There is also a distinct trade, called a horse's milliner; who makes roses for bridles, and other articles used in highly ornamented caparisons. This tradesman should have an inventive genius, and a considerable share of taste, to set off the furniture belonging to a horse, and decorate it in a neat and elegant style.

Saddler

THE SAWYER

Is a person who cuts the trunks of trees of various kinds into beams, planks, &c. for the use of carpenters and joiners, for the purposes of building.

The pit-saw, such as is represented in the plate, is a large two-handed saw, used to saw timber in pits. It is set rank for coarse stuff, so as to make a fissure of about a quarter of an inch wide.

The timber to be sawed is laid on a frame over an oblong pit, called a saw-pit, which is an improvement of modern times, as the power of a man standing in the pit must far exceed that which is exerted by him in a sitting posture. By means of a long saw, fastened in a frame, which is worked up and down by two men, one standing on the wood to be cut and the other in the pit, the operation of *sawing* is performed. As they proceed in their work, they drive wedges at a proper distance from the saw to keep the fissure open, which enables the saw to move with freedom.

This is a very laborious employment.

Sawyer

THE SHIPWRIGHT

Ships are built principally with *oak-timber*, which is the stoutest and strongest wood we have; and, therefore, best fitted both to keep sound under water, and to bear the blows and shocks of the waves, and the terrible strokes of cannon-balls. For this last purpose it is a peculiar excellence of the oak, that it is not so liable to splinter or shiver as other wood, so that a ball can pass through it without making a large hole.

The masts of ships are made of fir or pine, on account of the straightness and lightness of the wood.

During the construction of a ship she is supported in the dock, or upon a wharf, by a number of solid blocks of timber, placed at equal distances from, and parallel to, each other; in which situation she is said to be *on the stocks*.

In the plate the shipwright is represented standing at the stern, on a scaffold, and driving in the wedges with his wooden trunnel. The holes are first bored with the auger, and then the wedges driven in; these are afterwards cut off with a saw.

Shipwright

THE SMITH

There are at the present time, several branches in this trade: some are called black-smiths; of this class is the man represented in the plate: others are called *white-smiths*, or *bright smiths*; these polish their work to a considerable degree of nicety; some include in their business bell hanging, which is now carried to great perfection; others are chiefly employed in the manufacture of locks and keys.

In the smith's shop there must be a forge, an anvil and block, a vice fastened to an immoveable bench, besides hammers, tongs, files, punches, and pincers of different sorts.

The *forge* is the most prominent article; it is represented in the plate on the left hand of the smith. The forge is a sort of furnace, intended for heating metals so hot as to render them malleable, and fit to be formed into their various shapes.

In the front of the forge, but a little below it, is a *trough of water*, which is useful for wetting the coals to make them throw out a greater heat.

Smith

THE STATUARY

This Artist carves images and other ornaments in stone, marble, &c.

The art is one of those in which the ancients surpassed the moderns.

Statues are usually distinguished into four general kinds. The *first* are those less than life, of which kind are the statues of great men, or kings, and of the gods themselves. The *second* are those equal to the life; with these the ancients celebrated the deeds of men eminent for learning or valour. The *third* are those that exceed life; among which some surpassed the life once and a half; these were for monarchs and emperors, and those double the life for heroes. The *fourth* kind were still larger; these were called colossuses or colossal statues. Of this last the most eminent was the colossus of Rhodes, one of the wonders of the world, a brazen statue of Apollo, so high that ships passed in full sail between its legs. It was the workmanship of Chares, who spent twelve years in making it.

Statuary

THE STOCKING-WEAVER

The Stocking-weaver makes a part of the covering of the body worn in cold climates, including the foot, the leg, and a part of the thigh, commonly called stockings: the principal use of which is to defend those parts of the body from cold.

Formerly stockings were made of cloths, or of milled stuffs, sewed together: but, since the invention of knitting and weaving stockings of silk, wool, cotton, thread, &c. the use of cloth stockings has been entirely discontinued. In the year 1561, Queen Elizabeth was presented with a pair of black silk knit stockings, with which she was so much pleased, as to discontinue the use of those made of cloth.

It is a profitable business to the master; but journeymen must have considerable application to earn more than a guinea and a half a week. It is, however, clean neat work, and unexposed to the inclemencies of the weather. They are paid so much for each pair of stockings, and the price varies according to the fineness of the thread, cotton, silk, or worsted, of which they are manufactured.

Stocking-weaver

THE STONE-MASON

The business of a Stone-mason, consists in the art of hewing or squaring stone and marble; in cutting them for the purposes of building, and in being able to fix them in the walls of buildings with mortar.

The mason in the front of the plate is carving a stone with a *mallet* and *chisel*; before him, and on the block of the stone which supports the piece on which he is at work, lies the *bevel*: the two sides of the bevel move on a joint, so that they may be set to any angle. When masons or bricklayers speak of a bevel angle, they mean one which is neither forty-five nor ninety degrees.

In the back-ground of the picture there is a man sawing into thin pieces a large block of stone. The stone mason's saw is different from those used by other mechanics; it has no teeth; and being moved backwards and forwards by a single man, it cuts the stone by its own weight, and the friction occasioned by the motion.

Stone masons measure and charge for their work either by the superficial or cubic foot.

Stone-mason

THE TAILOR

In a tailor's shop, where much business is carried on, there are always two divisions of workmen: first, the foreman, who takes the measure of the person for whom the clothes are to be made, cuts out the cloth, and carries home the newly-finished garments to the customers. The others are mere working tailors, who sit cross-legged on the bench.

A writer on this subject says, that a master tailor ought to have a quick eye to steal the cut of a sleeve, the pattern of a flap, or the shape of a good trimming, at a glance: any bungler may cut out a shape when he has a pattern before him; but a good workman takes it by his eye in the passing of a chariot, or in the space between the door and a coach: he must be able not only to cut for the handsome and well-shaped, but bestow a good shape where nature has not granted it: he must make the clothes sit easy in spite of a stiff gait or awkward air: his hand and head must go together: he must be a nice cutter, and finish his work with elegance.

Tailor

THE TALLOW-CHANDLER

A tallow-candle to be good must be composed of sheep's and bullock's tallow. The wick ought to be pure, sufficiently dry, and properly twisted, otherwise the candle will emit an inconstant vibratory flame, which is both prejudicial to the eyes and insufficient for the distinct illumination of objects.

The tallow-chandler's business in London is generally performed in a cellar, of which, with the stairs down to it, we have a representation in the plate.

There are two sorts of tallow-candles; the one is dipped, the other moulded: the former are called common candles. The tallow is prepared by chopping the fat into small pieces, and then boiling it for some time in a large copper; when the tallow is extracted from the membranes by the boiling, the remainder is subjected to the operation of a strong iron press, and the cake that is left after the tallow is expressed from it, is called greaves; with this dogs are fed, and the greater part of the ducks that supply the London markets.

Tallow-chandler

THE TIN-PLATE WORKER

Tin-plate, or tin sheets, as they are usually called, is a composition of iron and tin, not melted together, but the iron in plates is dipped into a vessel of melted tin, or the iron in bars is covered over with tin, and then flatted or drawn out by means of mills.

The tin-plate worker receives the tinned sheets in boxes, containing a certain number. It is his business to form them into various articles, which are represented in the plate, such as kettles, saucepans, canisters of all sorts and sizes, milk pails, lanthorns, &c. &c.

The instruments that he makes use of, are a large pair of shears, to cut the tin into a proper size and shape, a polished anvil, and hammers of various kinds. The joints of his work he makes with *solder*, which is a composition of what is called *block-tin* and lead; this he causes to unite with the tin by means of rosin, and the application of heat, by an instrument of metal, formed for the purpose.

This business does not require great strength.

Tin-plate worker

THE TRUNK-MAKER

The persons employed in this trade make trunks, chests, portmanteaus, cases for holding plate and knives, and buckets.

Trunks, of which there are various shapes and sizes, are generally made of wood, and covered with leather, or the skins of horses or seals dressed with the hair on; and they are generally lined with paper. To some trunks, as that upon which the man is at work, represented in the plate, there are a number of thin iron cramps put on for the sake of strength.

Travelling trunks are fastened either before or behind the carriage with leathern straps and buckles, or by means of chains.

Portmanteaus are all of leather, and are adapted for the carriage, or may be placed behind the rider on his horse. These will contain a large quantity of linen clothes, and are very convenient for families.

The buckets hanging from the ceiling, are formed also of strong and stout leather, soaked and boiled. They are very useful for conveying water, in extinguishing houses that have taken fire.

Trunk-maker

THE TURNER

The art of turning is of great importance in a variety of trades and occupations, both useful and ornamental. The architect uses it for the ornaments both within and without highly-finished houses, and the mechanist and natural philosopher have recourse to it not only to embellish their instruments, but to adapt them to their different uses.

There are various kinds of lathes; that represented in the plate is as useful for small work as any. Some require the aid of one or two men to turn the wheel; but in this the wheel is turned by means of the treadle, by the same man who is employed in turning the wood. The thing to be turned is fixed on the lengthened axis of the smaller wheel, and upon the prop or rest, the chisel or other cutting instrument is supported; and being brought to touch the wood while it is swiftly turning round, it takes off shavings to the greatest nicety.

A journeyman in this business may earn a guinea and a half a week; and those who work on toys and smaller articles, much more.

Turner

THE WATCH-MAKER

The parts of a watch are made by several mechanics. The *movement-maker* forges the wheels in solid metal to the exact dimensions; from him they go to the person who cuts the teeth.

The wheels come back from the cutter to the movement-maker, who finishes them, and turns the corners of the teeth. The steel pinions are drawn at a mill, so that the watch-maker has only to file down the pivots, and fix them to the proper wheels.

The watch-springs form a trade of themselves: they are prepared by forming a very thin plate of steel into a double ring, binding it round with wire, and putting it in a proper furnace, to give it a suitable degree of heat. It is then dropped into oil or melted fat, which gives it a hardness equal to glass; it then undergoes several other operations, to bring it to that fine colour and polish which it possesses.

The chains are made principally by women, who cut them at a certain, and a small price per dozen.

Watch-maker

THE WEAVER

When the warp is mounted, the weaver treads alternately on the treadle, first on the right step, and then on the left, which raises and lowers the threads of the warp equally; between these he throws transversely the shuttle from one to the other; and every time that the shuttle is thus thrown, a thread of the woof is inserted in the warp. In this manner the work is continued till the piece is finished, that is, till the whole warp is filled with the woof; it is then taken off the loom by unrolling it from the beam, on which it had been rolled.

Journeymen weavers can, while in constant employ, make a good living. They will earn a guinea and a half or two guineas a week, according to the substance on which they are employed. It is a business that requires no great degree of strength, and a lad may be bound apprentice to it at twelve or thirteen years of age. Among weavers are found men of a thoughtful and literary turn. One of the first mathematicians of this country was Mr. Thomas Simpson, an industrious weaver in Spitalfields.

Weaver

THE WHEELWRIGHT

This artisan's employment embraces the making of all sorts of wheels for carriages which are employed in husbandry, as well as for those adapted to the purposes of pleasure. Road-waggons and other vehicles constructed for burden, are also the manufacture of the wheelwright.

The wheel is composed of several parts: as the *nave*, which is the centre-piece; the *spokes*, which are inserted at one end of the nave, and at the other, into the *fellies*, which make up the outside rim, or circumference of the wheel.

To the outside rim, or fellies, is an iron tire, fastened with very strong nails, or spikes. The parts of the tire are made red-hot before they are put on the wheels, in order that they may burn a small depth in the wheel, or, at least, all that roughness which might hinder it from lying flat with the wood: besides, being in this state, they may be easily bent, so as to conform most accurately to the curve of the wheel.

Wheelwrights in the country are makers also of carts, and a variety of other carriages.

Wheelwright

THE WIRE-DRAWER

The Wire-drawer reduces rods of different metals into smaller sizes, in order to render them proper for use in various trades, and for manufactures, and also many other purposes.

Metal wires are frequently drawn so fine, as to be wrought with other threads of silk, wool, or hemp; and thus they become a considerable article in the manufactures. The metals most commonly drawn into wire, are gold, silver, brass, copper, and iron.

The business of a wire-drawer is thus performed. If it be gold wire that is wanted, an ingot of silver is double gilt, and then, by the assistance of a mill, it is drawn into wire. The mill consists of a steel plate, perforated with holes of different dimensions, and a wheel which turns the spindles. The ingot, which at first is but small, is pressed through the largest hole, and then through one a degree smaller, and so continued, till it is drawn to the required fineness; and it is all equally gilt, if drawn out as fine as a hair.

Wire-drawer

THE WOOL-COMBER

The wool-comber cleanses and prepares wool in a proper state to be spun into worsted, yarn, &c. for weaving and other purposes.

The attitude of the wool-comber, in the plate, exhibits him in only one part of his business, the drawing out of the slivers. The wool intended for the manufacture of stuffs is brought into a state adapted for the making of worsted by the wool-comber. He first washes the wool in a trough, and, when very clean, puts one end on a fixed hook and the other on a moveable hook, which he turns round with a handle, till all the moisture is drained completely out. It is then thrown lightly out into a basket, such as is seen in the plate.

The wool-comber next throws it out very lightly into thin layers, on each of which he scatters a few drops of oil; it is then put together closely into a bin, which is placed under the bench on which he sits: at the back of the wool-bin is another and larger one, for what is called the noyles, that is, the part of the wool that is left on the comb after the sliver is drawn out.

Wool-comber

INDEX